VISITS BY OUR FRIENDS FROM THE "OTHER SIDE"

From the weekly diaries and recorded notes
of
Tom Harrison

CW00952860

*In memory of the Saturday Night Club Circle, now all in
the Spirit world; and in particular of Tom Harrison who
shared this knowledge with us and finally joined them
October 23rd 2010.*

© Saturday Night Press Publications

Copyright remains with the publisher. All rights reserved. No part of this book may be reproduced or utilised in any form or by any means electronic of mechanical without permission in writing from the publisher except for the purposes of reviewing or criticism as permitted under the Copyright Act of 1956

First Edition April 1989
ISBN 0 9514534 0 8

Revised Edition February 2011
ISBN 978 0 9557050 8 3

Saturday Night Press Publications
England

snppbooks@gmail.com

Printed by Lightning Source
www.lightningsource.com

DEDICATED

to my mother Minnie Harrison, my first wife Doris, and all those Spirit Friends and Helpers without whom this book could never have been written.

Publisher's Note:

This, Tom Harrison's original book is being reprinted by special request of several friends who like to give it to those they feel need its help.

Four years after Tom originally had this book printed he realised that he had omitted to mention anything about life in the Spirit world and so a folded loose sheet was inserted with each copy; the following year another sheet with the extract from Col. Dixon Smith's book was also added.

We have reproduced the book as Tom first set it up but with the two extra pieces now included in the book itself.

We hope that you enjoy it and if you wish to know more we hope you will read the larger book 'Life After Death: Living Proof '(2008) ISBN 09780955705014.

February 2011

CONTENTS

THE PURPOSE OF THIS BOOK

❖ To share with as many people as possible the wonderful experiences of our Family Home Circle in Middlesbrough from April 1946 to the mid 1950s; to interest those not actively involved in psychic matters and to help and encourage those who are.

❖❖ To pay tribute to my mother's remarkable mediumship and her many years of sacrifice for the benefit of so many other people, with no thought of personal gain whatsoever.

❖❖❖ To raise money for those admirable Charities dedicated to the nursing care of long-suffering victims of Cancer – which ravaged both my mother and my first wife for so many years.

Everyone who sat in our Circle was convinced of the genuineness of the exceptional phenomena they witnessed in such homely surroundings. Their personal thanks and letters said it all.

It happened as I have recounted it – without any financial or material gain ever being contemplated. My mother would have abhorred the very thought. Any motive therefore for deception, trickery or 'having to make something happen' was completely non-existent.

My personal notes made immediately after each weekly sitting are the major source of information for this book. What you will read are **Facts not Fiction**. Genuine eye-witness testimony.

For those interested in forming their own Home Circle may I offer the advice which we found so beneficial:-

Be strictly disciplined with your sitting arrangements

If you agree to start at 8pm – then start at 8pm, not 8.15 or 8.30 when it suits you. If you agree to sit every Saturday, or alternate Saturdays, or whenever – then do exactly what you have agreed. Your Spirit friends, with whom you are expecting to make contact, are at least entitled to such normally accepted courtesy; apart from the fact that they too have many preparations to make – especially with physical phenomena. There must be **complete sincerity** and **harmony of purpose** amongst the sitters; **each willing to give** for the benefit of the whole. **There is no place for egotists or self-seekers**. Give your room a friendly, cheerful and loving atmosphere, where your Spirit friends will be happy to accept your very warm welcome and make their presence felt in the manner they find most suitable at that time. As you progress always be ready, as we were, to make any changes they may advise.

Wishing you all success in your endeavours.

Tom Harrison

SETTING THE SCENE

A VERY warm welcome to our Home Circle. May I introduce our regular sitters whose sincere commitment made it all possible. Six of us started in April 1946, but we were soon joined by Mrs Hildred and Mr Jones making eight, who sat every week (except for an agreed annual holiday break) until the mid-1950s, when for health reasons my mother was unable to continue. She underwent many operations for cancer and passed over in 1958.

Our Medium – my mother, **Minnie Harrison**. The youngest of 10 children in the Bessant family who were all mediumistic in varying degrees. Parental encouragement enabled them to develop in an uninhibited environment and my mother was clairvoyant and clairaudient in her 'teenage' years. By the time we started our Home Circle she was 51 and had been a *trance medium* for some years. It was this type of phenomena therefore that we were anticipating when we started, but little did we know what wonderful and unexpected experiences were in store for us!

My father – **Thomas Henry Harrison** – known generally as Tosher. Not mediumistic but provided much psychic power.

Sydney and **Gladys Shipman** – our good friends and hosts when the sittings in our early years were held in their sitting room behind their baker's shop in Middlesbrough. A Master Baker and Company Director, Sydney was brought up in a Spiritualistic environment and is very mediumistic. A very practical type of man with a perceptive outlook – certainly not one given to self-deception or naivety. Gladys became interested in Spiritualism after they were married in 1937 and became a keen worker for the Movement. A good business woman and fellow Director in their Company. They now enjoy their retirement in Robin Hood's Bay, where, although in his mid-80's, Sydney still pursues his life-long enthusiasm for propounding our 'Psychic Truths'.

My first wife Doris, the second eldest of 10 in the *Hudson* family, a well known local Spiritualist family. A State Registered Nurse and Midwife, the devoted mother of our six children, Doris was quite mediumistic and very artistic but at the same time very practical and down to earth. A real family-woman, she was never happier than when surrounded by children.

Myself – an only child – brought up in a Spiritualistic environment where I met Doris. Modest healing powers with some mediumistic awareness, but more of a 'power-giver'. Like Sydney I have a 'no-nonsense' investigative outlook and cannot abide any semblance of pretension – especially when mediumship and psychic matters are involved. Member of Brit. Inst. Management.

Mrs Florence Hildred – Gladys' widowed mother whose husband *Sam* had passed over suddenly in December 1945. *Sam Hildred* soon became a first-class regular communicator through the trumpet. A most likeable and friendly man he obviously enjoyed his weekly chat. Spoke in a very clear voice and in his own unmistakable manner.

Mr William Brittain Jones, F.R.C.S. — a noted and highly respected surgeon in the North East; was Superintendent of Middlesbrough General Hospital for many years. An enthusiastic and lively man, with a wealth of investigative experience.

From the Spirit World – we had numerous helpers and regular visitors, but there were a *Special Few* whose guidance and support was particularly valuable, and whose names you will find occurring quite frequently throughout this book :–

Sunrise – a North American Indian – my mother's main Guide and our Circle Leader on the Spirit side. A completely dependable and faithful 'Chief' in every respect. He was the Organiser and Protector – the 'Link-man' in today's parlance – with specific responsibility for the safety of the medium from interfering or malevolent Spirits who do not understand the serious damage they can cause by their spontaneous actions. He 'stepped-in' on a number of occasions over the years.

Aunt Agg – (Mrs Agnes Abbott) – one of my mother's elder sisters who was a very well-known medium at the Marylebone Spiritualist Association (now the SAGB.) in London, from the mid-1930's until her passing to the Spirit world in 1942. Like my mother, a very homely and unassuming woman who always found the time to help those in need. A kindly person who would never speak ill of anyone, but strong enough to 'speak out' when needed.

Granny Lumsden – Doris's grandmother on her mother's side; passed to the Spirit world in 1930 in her mid-70s. Another one who used to spend most of her time here looking after the needs of others. A warm and friendly personality who always materialised with a spontaneous laugh and cheery word for everyone. Never a dull moment when Granny was around!

Sam Hildred – see Mrs Hildred above.

THE diagram below shows how the seating was arranged for our weekly sittings. My mother sat in front of the rolled up curtain for the **Trumpet Voice** phenomena and then when the curtain was unrolled moved to the chair behind it for the **Materialisation** phenomena. The reasons for this are explained later.

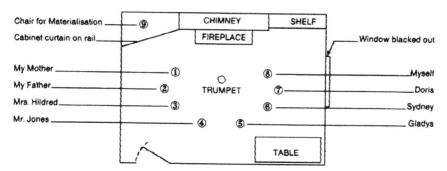

We always opened with a prayer – in our case the 'Invocation To Angels' from a book called *The Lyceum Manual* with which we were familiar – but any other sincere prayer asking for protection and guidance during the sitting would suffice.

Then we would join hands for a few minutes and sing four or five bright and cheerful songs we all knew. This helps to 'raise the vibrations' to assist our Spirit friends. We sat in a completely relaxed mood using the chairs in the room – some lounge, some diners. It is extremely important to create a friendly, welcoming atmosphere at all times and both love and laughter are timely ingredients.

In the early days we sat in complete darkness throughout the whole sitting – usually no longer than an hour – but as we developed the sittings took on a different format – first the **trumpet** phenomena followed later by the **materialisations.** During the trumpet phenomena, an ectoplasmic rod is connected from the medium to the smaller end of the trumpet *(as seen in Photograph C)*. This enables the Spirit helpers to move the trumpet around the room as well as being the 'telephone line' along which the Spirit voices are transmitted for everyone in the room to hear. In effect the trumpet is an amplifying megaphone.

As will be seen from the diagram, the aluminium trumpet was placed on a board on the floor in the centre of the Circle. Being in complete darkness, we were unable to see much movement of it during our earliest sittings but we could certainly hear the 'knocking' our Spirit friends made with it on the board. In fact, because of their regular knocking – often with great force – the soft aluminium bell-end became quite misshapen and Sydney affixed a stronger band of thicker metal which is there to this day. This trumpet was in fact the one which was used in *Aunt Agg's* own Home Circle before her passing – she too had been a good *trumpet medium.*

By our tenth sitting we had developed sufficiently for our Spirit helpers to tell us we could have luminous spots on the bell-end so that we were then able to clearly see its movement around the room.

When the trumpet phenomena began, usually within five or six minutes of starting, many Spirit friends would indicate their presence with different movements of the trumpet. Then *Sunrise* would indicate his presence and control by rapidly moving the bell-end in circles – the sign of the Sun. Within a few minutes the trumpet would be brought to rest in a horizontal position about five feet above the floor; perfectly still in the centre of the Circle.

The voices would then emanate from there – sometimes loud and clear, sometimes barely audible – depending on the ability of the Spirit communicator. *Sam Hildred* was always very clear and forceful – exactly the same as when he was here on the Earth. *Sunrise's* voice was also quite clear and generally he acted as the *Master of Ceremonies*, telling us who would be speaking next. Over the years his command of the English language improved considerably much to his satisfaction and pleasure.

As I have said, our sittings then developed into the **two parts – trumpet and materialisation**. It was usually after about half an hour that *Sunrise* would tell us it was time for the 'changeover' and he would return the trumpet to its original place on the board. After about five minutes Mam had come sufficiently out of her deep trance to be able to move to the chair in the corner – but often needed some help to take the few steps.

The piece of black-out curtaining, which had been folded over the wooden rail, would then be dropped across the corner and my mother would be sitting in a very simple 'cabinet'. We would then switch on the subdued red light, to which a rheostat had been fitted so that I could adjust the brightness, depending on the experience and ability of the Materialised Spirit people.

As we developed further, certain Spirit people who came each week – like *Aunt Agg and Granny Lumsden* – were able to withstand a much brighter light and stay much longer – often up to 10/15 minutes. Photograph 'B' was taken in such a bright red light.

After Mam had gone into the cabinet we then sang a few more cheerful songs to help re-build the power. Within a few minutes *Sunrise* would speak to us from behind the curtain by means of **Direct Voice** i.e. without the trumpet but **through an ectoplasmic voice box**. This would indicate that Mam was again in deep trance and the materialisations would proceed.

At the beginning, our sittings seldom exceeded an hour, but within a few months they were often one and a half to two hours – depending on the 'power' available – and the timing was always in the hands of our Spirit helpers. *Sunrise* would tell us when it was time to close and we would respond accordingly.

Over a bite of supper, provided by Gladys each week, we would eagerly discuss what had happened and I would immediately make my brief weekly notes. **My mother** always listened with great interest of course, and often amazement, because, being in deep trance she **was completely unaware of anything that had happened.**

All of us thanked her every week for giving us so much joy and pleasure without being able to partake of it herself. Her modest and truly humble reply was always in the same vein – that she didn't really do anything; it was *Aunt Agg, Sunrise and all the other Spirit helpers who did the work*! She was 'only' the medium and just went to sleep!

In the early '50s we were fortunate enough to be given a tape recorder (still quite a novelty in those days) by Doris's mother, Mrs Annie Hudson, a truly gracious and lovable lady. Then my mother had the added pleasure of listening to the recordings as we played them back each week while having supper. Unfortunately we were unable to afford sufficient new tapes to be able to keep every recording, so usually over-recorded each week. **They were mainly for my mother's benefit – and she certainly enjoyed them,** especially when Spirit people like her sisters and brothers and other friends were able to leave specific messages for her to listen to. I do still have one or two special recordings which we kept.

But please remember – and it cannot be repeated too often – such communication is very much a two-way affair and time and time again our Spirit friends have thanked us for giving them the opportunity to meet and speak to their loved ones still on the Earth.

We never 'bring them back' – they are always amongst us – ever welcoming the opportunity to make their presence known to us, in their own individual ways which we are able to recognise.

They live very active lives in the Spirit world without the encumbrance of a physical body and never intrude on the privacy of our everyday living; but are readily on hand when we feel the desire or need to call on them – never more than a thought away!

THE WAY HOME

O N Saturday evening, 10th January 1948, we all heard this soft and rather hesitant voice coming through the trumpet which was suspended in the centre of our Circle.

It belonged to a boy who gave his name as *James Andrew Fletcher*. He had passed over when he was about *12 years old* and had been attracted to our Circle by the 'bright light' emanating from it, whilst we were sitting in a darkened room.

By a series of questions and answers we obtained as much information as possible, but he was still rather unsure of himself. We gathered that *he had passed over on 6th June 1941; had no brothers or sisters but did have a pet dog* of which he was very fond.

He thought he had lived in Coniston Avenue, or something like that, in Haverton Hill, which is a village a few miles from Middlesbrough alongside the vast ICI. Billingham Works. He had tried to visit his home, he said, but there seemed to be a mist which he could not get through.

Was it near us and could we help him?

I was free the following Wednesday afternoon and told him I would go to Haverton Hill to see if I could find his home, and invited him to accompany me – with the help of perhaps *Aunt Agg* or other Spirit people familiar to him.

We would try to penetrate that misty barrier and link him again with his mother and father – and his pet dog, if still there.

Not knowing Haverton Hill at all well, I stopped my car at a local shop. Did they know a Coniston Avenue? No, sorry – but there is a Collinson Road just around the corner. I thanked them and drove round.

In front of me was a long road of council houses, four or five to a block, with small front gardens – similar to thousands built in the 1930's. I stood there wondering where to start my enquiries – which were unusual to say the least. **'Collinson' – 'Coniston' – they were similar, so I MUST have a try, for James's sake.**

Three o'clock on a Wednesday afternoon and not a soul in sight. Which door do I knock on? The answer was given to me when I saw a lady coming out of her house about three blocks away.

"Excuse me, but could you tell me where the Fletchers live, please?" Imagine my surprise when she immediately replied – "Oh yes, just on the corner there at No 20." Could it be as easy as this I thought?

I rang the bell at No 20. No reply. I rang again. Still no reply, but a lady appeared at the door of the adjoining house. Could she help?

"Yes please – I was wanting to speak to Mrs Fletcher." MRS automatically came to my mind as I thought she was more likely to be at home at that time of the day. Mr. would no doubt be working."

"No, she is out at present – works at the ICI canteen and won't be home until about 4.30." I thanked her and said I would try to return about 7.30 and perhaps she would mention it to Mrs Fletcher.

Around 7.30 I did return – a pitch black and extremely cold January night, with very dim gas street lighting.

Again I rang the bell at No. 20 – rather more apprehensively this time, wondering what was ahead of me. This time there was a reply, quite quickly, and a man confronted me at the door.

"Are you the chap who came to see my wife this afternoon?" he barked at me before I had time to speak! Oh dear I thought – what have I done!

"Yes sir," I replied, as friendly as possible, "but I would also like to speak to you if I may."

"Well, what do you want?" he snapped.

As I have said, my enquiries were rather unusual, without such an opening confrontation. Ah well, I thought, here goes – just ask simple questions and play it by ear.

"Did you have a son called James Andrew?" "Yes," came the reply.

"Was he about 12 years old when he died?" Another curt, "Yes."

"Did he die on 6th June 1941?" I asked, now feeling quite inwardly excited.

"Yes," he said again, not quite so aggressively this time – but quickly added – "How do YOU know, and what's this all about?" A very reasonable question to put to a complete stranger who knocks on your door on a dark winter's night.

"I'm researching some information about psychic phenomena and was hoping that you may be able to assist me," I replied.

Little did he realise how much he had already done so. **Three questions – Three affirmatives!**

All this, still at the front door, in the space of three or four minutes.

Had I really found the home of that 'voice' which we had all heard for the first time only four days previously? It certainly seemed like it – but more was yet to come. By this time a lady had appeared at the doorway.

"What's happening? What does he want?" she asked. Mr Fletcher explained briefly but in a much more subdued voice, and without the original aggression.

"Well would you like to come in and talk?" said the lady, and I seemed to detect a sense of expectancy in her voice. "Many thanks – it is rather cold tonight out here."

From the moment we entered their living room the atmosphere seemed to change – much friendlier, although still rather apprehensive.

A cheerful open fire greeted us and I sat in an armchair next to the sideboard, on which was *a framed photograph of a good looking boy – surely James*. Mr and Mrs Fletcher sat on the settee on the other side of the fireplace facing me – still a complete stranger asking questions about their dead son. But the friendliness continued. "Would you like a cup of tea?" "Many thanks," I replied.

As Mrs Fletcher went through to the kitchen a **rough-haired terrier** bounded out and immediately sat down in front of me; tail wagging vigorously, ears pricked and whining rather than barking. "Most unusual," remarked Mr Fletcher, "he's not usually so friendly with strangers."

But as I explained to them, he wasn't looking directly at me, rather over my right shoulder where no doubt James was standing behind me. **Yes, this was James's dog, 'Rags', and he was welcoming him home!**

Mission accomplished I thought – and I would be leaving after I had enjoyed my cup of tea, But not so.

As Mrs Fletcher handed me the cup of tea she rather diffidently said, "We're Catholics, you see," with all the attendant implications. I immediately offered to leave and assured them I had no intention of offending their religious beliefs or principles.

"Oh no," she said, "we would like to talk to you," and her husband nodded in agreement. From then on Mrs Fletcher did most of the talking – a mother's natural love for her only child being very evident.

I explained briefly about our small group and how we had heard their son's voice last Saturday evening. They listened intently and with obvious interest. There was certainly no indication of any feeling of disbelief.

Although it was a few days past 'Twelfth Night', I noticed there were still a few Christmas decorations in the room – but that is not unusual. **What was unusual however, was the reason they were there at all.**

During our talk, **Mrs Fletcher told me she had a 'strange' feeling around Christmas time** to get a tree and decorate the room as they had always done when James was alive. The feeling was so strong, although she had no idea why, that she unpacked all the decorations which they had put away and never used since James died – over six years ago.

She now realised, she said, why the feeling was so strong this particular year and felt so very pleased that she had done it!

I now felt that my visit had not only been instrumental in getting James back to his home, but equally important, his mother and father were aware of his presence and happily accepted the situation. *The 'mist' which James had been unable to penetrate had now been lifted and the Fletcher family was again complete.*

The 'bright light' that James had seen emanating from our Circle on that Saturday evening had been as a beacon to him, and he came to thank us the following Saturday – this time in a much stronger and clearer voice!

That same bright psychic light was also a beacon to many other frustrated, confused or simply 'lost' Spirits whom we were so pleased to help over the years.

SPECIAL NOTE

This is **evidence of Spirit survival of the highest quality** because James came to us that evening as a complete stranger and **none of us knew anything about him or his family.**

Yet I was able to follow the sketchy information he gave us and **prove conclusively that it was 100 per cent accurate.**

The overworked excuse/reason so often used by the sceptics that mediums obtain their information from the sitters' minds, without their realising it, **just could not apply in this case.**

James's joy, and that of his parents, was matched by ours at being able to help them all in such a positive manner.

(For reasons of personal privacy the surname and road name has been changed, but all the rest is exactly as it happened)

ECTOPLASMIC MATERIALISATIONS –
NOT Ghostly Apparitions

A S you will see from the Photographs 'A', 'B' and 'C', **ectoplasm is a material substance** emanating from the medium. It is used by the Spirit helpers – chemists and scientists – in many ways and is in effect their 'building material'. It is affected by light of any kind, especially white light, and this is why much of this type of phenomena is witnessed in either complete darkness or dim red light.

Critics and sceptics regularly use this as a 'weapon' to attack the genuineness of such phenomena, but conveniently seem to forget that we would have no prints of photographic negatives if these were processed in white light. As in photography, a red light is often used in materialisation circles like ours, but only with the consent of the Spirit helpers. This is extremely important for the protection of the medium who could be severely injured by the use of an unexpected source of light – especially the likes of a torchlight. Such irresponsible actions were a contributory factor in the death of the well known materialisation medium, Helen Duncan, and it was our responsibility as sitters to ensure that my mother was never in such danger.

Although we sat in complete darkness for the first six months, it did not mean we were unable to see some of the phenomena in the room as our eyes gradually adjusted to perceive things close to us – and in such a small room nothing was more than four or five feet away from each of us.

But better still – on 23rd November 1946 – we were told by Sunrise that we could have a subdued red light, thus enabling us to see things even more clearly.

We had been having materialised hands for a number of weeks and our Spirit helpers told us they were gradually developing the skills required by them to eventually have fully materialised spirit people. On the 7th December 1946, to our great delight and not a little wonderment, they achieved their aim and my *Aunt Agg* materialised!

Clearly visible to all the sitters, in the subdued red light, she stood in the centre of the Circle, leaned towards me and held my hand – quite firmly and naturally. She then handed me three pink carnations and one white one, which I well recall gripping so very tightly – fearing I suppose that they would disappear. But of course, like all the other apports we received, they did not do so, and I still have one of them in my collection (Photo 'D').

It was a very moving and significant evening, but only the beginning of so many more exciting and pleasurable evenings to follow.

For the following six weeks we had no trumpet phenomena whatsoever, but a number of different Spirit people materialised at each sitting in the subdued red light. Our Spirit helpers were making excellent progress and during all these sittings my mother was sitting in the circle (chair No.1 in the diagram) in full view of all of us. This meant that **we could all see both the Medium and the materialised Spirit at one and the same time!**

I should perhaps explain that throughout the years of our Home Circle, although we had many materialisations at each sitting, only **one** Spirit materialised at any one time because there was only one ectoplasmic cord/link with the medium.

One week *Mr Jones' mother materialised* and they held each other's hands for a few minutes. Before she left we all heard her say to him – "Brittain my boy", which he later confirmed, rather emotionally for Mr Jones, was what she always called him. No one else in the room knew that, and certainly not my mother, the medium – although of course, we did know that Brittain was part of his full name.

When we were chatting over supper afterwards, Mr Jones remarked that, being a Doctor, he would very much like to feel the pulse of Aunt Agg's materialised body sometime and we agreed to mention it during our sitting the following Saturday.

Come the following Saturday evening. Aunt Agg materialised as usual. But before we had any time to say anything to her about Mr Jones' request, she turned directly towards him, held out her arm and said she had come that night with the express purpose of letting him feel her pulse!

Another example of the closeness and friendliness of our Spirit helpers who had evidently still been amongst us while we were having our supper and overheard Mr Jones' remarks.

Mr Jones was delighted of course to have such an immediate response and there and then felt her pulse, He confirmed that it was quite normal and then added in his typically dry humorous manner. **"Thank you, Mrs Abbott** (which he always called my Aunt) **you'll live all right."** *Aunt Agg* chuckled and assured us that he was absolutely right – **she is still very much alive!**

Early in January 1947, *Sunrise* told us that the 'building process' of the materialised forms in the subdued red light was taking so much 'power' that it was doubtful if we would ever be able to increase the illumination much more. We had discussed this with him on many occasions and he now suggested that we improvise a simple 'cabinet' to protect the 'building process' from the red light. Then, he said, the Spirit people could build more effectively in the cabinet and then come forward into our view in a much brighter red light.

From this you will appreciate our positive outlook and attitude towards any possible improvement of the phenomena. By the following Saturday evening therefore Sydney had fixed a length of 'black-out' curtain material (in plentiful supply immediately after the war) to a suitable length of wood and arranged for it to rest on the picture rail across the corner alcove to the left hand side of the fireplace. *(See 'Setting the Scene' & Photo 'B'.)*

This very simple arrangement was extremely effective and remained as our 'cabinet' throughout the many years of our sittings. The 15-inch gap above the curtain to the ceiling held no problems for our Spirit helpers. In fact, as we developed, extremely bright flashes of white light were created by them behind the curtain and because of the gap we were all able to witness them. *(See later chapter 'Spirit Lights').*

From our first sitting with the cabinet on 18th January 1947, the 'quality' of the materialised forms improved significantly and they were able to stay with us much longer. **Frequently Aunt Agg would sit on the empty chair in front of the cabinet and stay for up to 10 minutes – with occasional visits lasting 15 minutes** (all as recorded in my note books). These longer stays were usually when we had special visitors like her son Terry, her sister Mary or close friends she had known in Middlesbrough years ago before her move to London.

Spirit people materialising for the first time said they found great difficulty in supporting the weight of the ectoplasmic body and robes – especially those who had been in the Spirit world for many years. They likened it to our being clothed in a thick heavy overcoat with the pockets loaded with heavy weights – not the easiest of things to stand up or walk around in.

Generally the 'newcomers' would move the curtain to one side and stand alongside the fireplace – like *Aunt Agg* in Photo 'B'. I would then go across the room to greet them, shake hands or embrace and kiss them if they were relatives or close friends. When we had materialised Spirits for visitors to our Circle I would take them to meet each other and they too would generally embrace and kiss each other.

At the end of their visits the more experienced materialised Spirits, like Aunt Agg and Granny Lumsden, would simply bid us farewell in their own way and step back behind the curtain.

Those not so experienced however were unable to do this because of the difficulties with the unfamiliar weight of the ectoplasm. After standing and talking to us for a few minutes they would usually say something to the effect that they "couldn't hold up any longer" and would have to go. Whilst they were still talking to us the ectoplasmic body would gradually sink towards the floor and appear to be going through a 'trap-door' – which I can assure you was not there in Syd and Gladys's carpeted living room

What in fact was happening was that owing to their inability to hold the 'power', the ectoplasm was gradually moving backwards along the floor, into the cabinet and towards the medium, to whom it was connected at all times. These Spirits were frequently heard to be expressing their frustration and disappointment as they gradually disappeared, but we were assured by our Spirit helpers that neither the materialised Spirit nor the medium suffered any ill effects because the whole procedure was completely under their control.

As you will have gathered, **materialised Spirits are not ghostly apparitions**. They are people from the Spirit world – who are still very close to us, very interested in helping us when needed, and always very, very pleased to have the opportunity to meet us in such a tangible way. Compare it with the feelings of an elderly grandmother in the UK. able to fly, for the very first time perhaps, to her children and grandchildren who had emigrated to Australia 30 or 40 years ago.

Whilst every sitting was always special to us and we never took anything for granted – there were a number of occasions when something quite unexpected or very different occurred and these I have recounted in more detail in individual stories, a few of which are included in this book.

The Beyond.

It seemeth such a little way to me across to that strange country — the Beyond,
And yet not strange, for it has grown to be the home of those of whom I am so fond.

Ella Wheeler Wilcox

AUNT AGG'S BIRTHDAY ANNIVERSARY
AND HER SON'S WEDDING DAY

SATURDAY 14th June 1947 was a rather special day for Aunt Agg. It would have been her 62nd birthday anniversary (she died in November 1942) – and on this day her youngest son Terry was married to one of my wife's younger sisters, Ruby Hudson, at the Middlesbrough Spiritualist Church.

The wedding ceremony was conducted by a long-standing friend of both the Hudson family and *Aunt Agg* – Jim McKenzie – known to everyone as Mac. The organist was another good friend – Mr. Todd. It was fitting therefore that Mr and Mrs McKenzie and Mr and Mrs Todd had been invited as visitors to our Home Circle that particular evening. The phenomena for both couples proved to be very exciting and evidential!

We started in our usual way with trumpet voice phenomena. The first voice we heard was very faint – just "Bruce. . . Bruce. . ." and nothing more. Our Spirit leader *Sunrise* then took control of the trumpet and told us that the voice belonged to a young boy who was accompanied by another boy whose names were Bruce and Robert. He then added that 'burning' was connected with both of their passings to the Spirit world but they were unable to use the trumpet to speak to us themselves.

Mr and Mrs Mackenzie immediately recognised them as their son Bruce and his cousin Robert. Robert had been burned to death some years ago as a boy, and Bruce had been so badly scalded in an accident in their home when he was only 11 months old that he passed to the Spirit world.

Bruce's accident had happened nine years ago while Mac had been attending to him, and ever since that sad day he had blamed himself for not keeping a closer watch. Sunrise then told Mac that Bruce wanted his father to know that he must not blame himself and that Bruce knew how much he had suffered over the past nine years. This certainly appeared to ease Mac's mind, as he said at the time.

But better still, later during the sitting, Bruce materialised as a young man who had grown up in the Spirit world. He was able to talk to his father face-to-face and comfort him in the most personal way possible. Although Mac had experienced materialisation phenomena previously, on this special occasion he was quite overcome – but went home a very happy father indeed.

I could not help thinking at the time just how wonderful it would be if only the countless number of grieving parents, relatives and close friends were able to put themselves in Mac's shoes. The world would be a much happier place, I'm sure.

After *Sunrise* had told us about Bruce and Robert another gentleman then spoke through the trumpet – said he was also James McKenzie, Mac's father. He spoke quite clearly, with a slight Scottish accent and in short clipped phrases. More good evidence was given to Mac from his father. Later *Sunrise* said that Mac had felt very bitter about the way his father had acted whilst on the earth, but recently had forgiven him as he felt he had 'worked out his own salvation'.

Mac immediately confirmed this was absolutely true – but we in the Circle had certainly not been aware of it. His father had left his wife and their children when Mac was only six years old – a fact known only to the McKenzies in that room that evening! It is interesting to recall that at another sitting months later when

Mac was a visitor again, his father materialised and they met face to face. Whilst they stood together shaking hands and talking, his father begged forgiveness. In a very emotional moment for both of them, Mac had no hesitation in offering that forgiveness.

After more trumpet phenomena we had our usual materialisations with a number of Spirit relatives for our visitors. When Mrs Todd's mother materialised she appeared quite upset because her other daughter was apparently very ill. Again this was confirmed by Mrs Todd and of the people in the room that night, only Mr and Mrs Todd were aware of that. Her mother assured her that they were helping as much as they possibly could.

Finally *Aunt Agg materialised* – as always, closing the evening's sitting with her cheerful and friendly presence. As she stepped forward from the cabinet, we could all see in the fairly bright red light that **she was holding five carnations in her hand** and she was clearly so full of joy to be able to hand them out with her usual well chosen and suitable words.

One to Mac –"for conducting the ceremony today that meant so much to her."

One to Mr Todd – "for playing the organ so well."

One to my wife Doris to pass on to her sister Ruby, today's bride – "With all my love and best wishes."

One to Mrs Mac – "an old dear friend."

One to Mrs Todd, to whom she said – "I think I knew you as Effie, didn't I, back in St Pauls Road?" – and Mrs Todd immediately agreed with her. She told us later that that was over 15 years ago when *Aunt Agg* had lived in St Pauls Road in Middlesbrough – and even more significant – only Mrs Todd herself knew that – not even her husband.

Aunt Agg then expressed a mother's pleasure about her youngest son marrying such a lovely girl who would look after him and that he had 'joined' such a good, close-knit family. Just before she went I wished her many happy returns of the day and she replied by saying it was the happiest birthday she had ever had.

Another very happy evening which was so thoroughly enjoyed by everyone involved – particularly Aunt Agg and our Spirit friends!

And there are Spirits, messengers of Love.
Who come at call and fortify our Strength.

Ella Wheeler Wilcox.

*   *   *   *

Thoughts do not need the wings of words to fly to any goal,
Like subtle lightnings, not like birds,
They speed from soul to soul.

Ella Wheeler Wilcox.

WE LIVE

(These verses were given through the mediumship of my mother in 1954. They were composed by her brother in the Spirit world, Jack Bessant, who was killed in a works accident in the mid-1920s and often spoke to us through the trumpet.)

Mourn not for me my loved ones, For I am by your side,
I have not sped to realms unknown or crossed the rolling tide.
I do not leave you comfortless – think not I ever will;
So dry those tears, look up and smile, for I am with you still.

My eyes once closed are opened, my vision clear and bright;
Where once I looked through darkened glass, I see perpetual light.
The veil has just been lifted and my loved ones gone before
Are waiting now to welcome me, as in the days of yore.

Their love is still enfolding me, Their spirits have not fled;
And now I know as I am known – WE LIVE! There are no dead!
So let your hearts be comforted, cast out all doubt and fear;
We live and walk beside you – your loved ones still are near.

Grieve not for me my dear ones, just dry those tears away;
I'll walk with you through Earth's dark night until the break of day.
So lift your hearts in thankful praise and join with us to sing –
Oh, Grave where is thy victory? Oh, Death where is thy sting?

*　　　　*　　　　*　　　　*

The voice of the dead was a living voice to me.

Alfred, Lord Tennyson.

*　　　　*　　　　*　　　　*

THE HOMEWARD ROAD

(One of the many poems written on odd sheets of paper found amongst my mother's belongings after her passing in 1958.)

You have passed beyond our sight along the unseen way,
On the homeward journey that we all must take some day.

In heart and home you leave a gap that no-one else can fill,
You have gone – and yet it seems that you are near us still

You're only just a step ahead around the hidden bend –
On the road that leads us homeward to our journey's end

Though the sorrows of bereavement linger in our mind,
Happy is the memory that you have left behind.

PHOTOGRAPHS

PHOTOGRAPHS 'A', 'B' and 'C' on the following pages, were all taken during sittings in our Home Circle **with the complete co-operation of our Spirit helpers. This is of paramount importance.**

Our sole purpose when we discussed the idea with *Aunt Agg* and *Sunrise*, was for my mother to be able to see something of the wonderful phenomena which we were privileged to experience each week. Being in deep trance she was completely unaware of what was happening. The thought of publication never entered our heads.

When approval was given for a specific sitting, we set up the camera on a tripod, pre-set the 'stop' and focus and pointed it in the direction of the place where the phenomena would occur. **It was all very much 'hit and miss', with the hope that we might be fortunate enough to get something.**

We were amazed and delighted when we achieved such splendid results – especially with those taken in complete darkness. Those were taken on infra-red plates with an 'flash' exposure of a Sashalight bulb housed in a wooden box which had a two inches square Wratten ruby-red filter set into the front cover. I still have the box, made by Sydney, amongst my memorabilia — together with a carton of unused infra-red plates.

Compared with today's 'hi-tech' equipment it seems almost 'pre-historic' – but that was 40 years ago and we were only amateur photographers at the best of times. I think the three I have selected are the most interesting and evidential of the dozen or so we took.

'A' – ECTOPLASM EMANATING FROM THE MEDIUM

Taken in December 1948, in complete darkness, with a Kodak infra-red plate.

My mother is in deep trance sitting on a chair in the corner of the room, which, with the black curtain seen in Photo 'B' formed the very simple cabinet which assisted the 'building process' of the materialised Spirit people. The ectoplasm is emanating from her mouth and in this form it is quite transparent, very similar in appearance and texture to chiffon.

I must admit that when my mother first saw this photograph she was rather taken aback and somewhat queasy to think that this was happening to her whilst she was 'asleep'. But it did not deter her from sitting for many years to come – thus giving so much joy and pleasure to so many people, both here and in the Spirit world.

This photograph in particular clearly illustrates how much the medium places herself in the hands of the sitters and the paramount need for protection at such times. This I cannot stress too often.

'A' (Left)
Ectoplasm emanating from the medium's mouth.

Taken in complete darkness using a Kodak infra-red plate.

Exposure by means of powerful 'Sashalight' bulb through a Wratten glass filter - extremely deep ruby-red colour.

Taken in December 1948.

(Ref. page 13 & 19)

'B'(Right)
Fully materialised ectoplasmic Spirit person – in this case Aunt Agg (mother's sister).

Taken in red light using fast Kodak film. Two minutes exposure.

Taken in February 1948.

(Ref. page 13,15 & 22)

'C'(Right)
Shows how the
trumpet is
operated by Spirit
helpers using
ectoplasmic rod.

Method of
exposure the same
as in 'A' with
infra-red plate.

Taken in
December 1948.

(Ref. page 8 & 22)

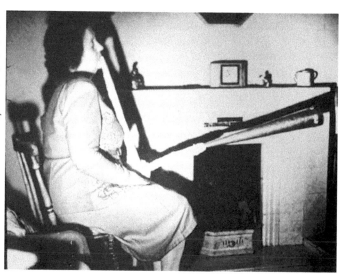

'D'(Left)
A few of the many hundreds of apports we received.

These and many others particularly flowers are still in my possession.

(Ref. page 23, 26 &31)

'E'(Right)
The two Indian-style
bells mentioned in the
account of our sitting
on 5th January 1948.

(Ref. page24)

'B' – FULLY MATERIALISED ECTOPLASMIC SPIRIT PERSON

Taken in February 1948, in a subdued red light with a 'superfast' film and exposure time of two minutes.

This is my *Aunt Agg* and as you can see, she stood perfectly still. The man to the left is my father, one of the sitters, and you can see from the double exposure that he actually moved during the two minutes. Also during the exposure time we heard my mother moving on her chair behind the curtain. *Aunt Agg* then told us during her five or six minutes stay afterwards, that Mam had been 'suspended' in the opposite corner of the room looking down at *Aunt Agg* and had been trying to reach her – hence the movement.

She added that after the Circle, Mam would probably recall this experience – and she did just that, during supper, when she suddenly said – "Oh, I saw our Agg tonight, standing here by the fireplace" – pointing to the exact place.

"I was up there in that corner," she added, without any prompting from us, and pointed to the opposite corner which *Aunt Agg* had indicated previously. "She looked just as she always was – it was lovely!" This had been a unique experience for my mother and she had obviously enjoyed it.

You will observe differences in the texture of the ectoplasm e.g. the face, the upper part of the robe, and the lower part which is similar to Photograph 'A'. I usually moved across the room to greet our Spirit friends and can assure you that the hands and faces were exactly the same as human flesh – quite smooth and warm. All our visitors who shared this wonderful experience of embracing their loved ones always confirmed the naturalness of the materialised Spirits – nothing distasteful and certainly nothing to be afraid of.

'C' – MANIPULATION OF TRUMPET BY ECTOPLASMIC ROD.

Taken in December1948, in complete darkness with a Kodak infra-red plate; same as Photo 'A'.

This shows the 'mechanics' of trumpet voice phenomena on a cantilever principle. The ectoplasmic 'rod', so solid that you can clearly see the shadow behind it, emanates from the medium's mouth (as in 'A') and although the Spirit people make use of the medium's voice box whilst she is in deep trance, their voices are all quite different – as they were when here on the Earth.

The other end of the 'rod' is attached to the smaller end of the trumpet, thus enabling the Spirit people to move it around the room in mid-air. When they were speaking through the trumpet it was usually 'suspended', perfectly still, about five feet from the floor in the centre of the circle – from which position we could normally hear their voices quite clearly. But when we had a visitor who was rather hard of hearing, the trumpet would be moved closer to that person. **Another indication of the ever present awareness of our Spirit friends!**

'D' – SOME OF THE APPORTS WE RECEIVED

A few examples of the hundreds of apports we received at our Saturday night sittings. In our early sittings they were usually found in the room after we closed – small flowers having been dropped on to our knees and larger flowers often found on the hearth. Later, when we had full materialised Spirit people (as in photo B) the apports were frequently handed to the recipient by the materialised Spirits themselves.

These examples, together with some others, are still in my possession, and these are recent photographs taken specifically for this publication by Alan Harrison, one of my sons.

In the plastic envelope is a dried Carnation. The four metallic items are

[i] A Spiritualist Lyceum lapel badge with the picture of the founder Andrew Jackson Davis. This was brought by an old pioneer of the Middlesbrough Lyceum – Mr. Chas Roeder when he materialised at our Children's Party sitting on 3rd January 1948.

[ii] A Royal Artillery uniform button brought during our "Soldiers' Night" sitting on 8th November, 1947 which was the nearest Saturday to Armistice Day. We always paid our respects by holding such a sitting at this time each year, when the majority of our Spirit visitors were Servicemen from both World Wars.

On this particular night one of them was a youngster whom my father had befriended at Ypres – Billy Earle. My father felt so emotionally moved by his tragic death at the age of 17, he decided when I was born in 1918 to remember young Billy by adding William to the family name of Thomas – hence my name of Thomas William. The poppy was also brought one soldiers' night.

[iii] A damaged Queen Victoria penny dated 1864, 'aported' one Saturday evening from a box of old coins which I kept in a drawer at home, about half a mile away. I still have the box with all the other coins in it.

[iv] A Canadian 5-cent piece which was only our second apport brought during Sitting 5 on 18th May 1946.

'E' – THE TWO INDIAN-STYLE BELLS mentioned in the story below of our Christmas Party Sitting, in January 1954. The smaller one was ours with a broken prong. The larger one was the Apport, which was certainly not in the room when we started the sitting but was there when we finished.

OUR CHRISTMAS PARTY AND THE TWO INDIAN-STYLE BELLS

DURING the Christmas and New Year period each year we held a special sitting which we called the Spirit Children's Party. Our own family Christmas tree was taken into the Circle room and the decorations included many small toys such as dolls, cars, aeroplanes, bags of sweets etc.

Every year we had a splendid evening with a happy party atmosphere and lots of activity by our Spirit friends. Many of the presents were taken from the tree by the Spirit children, not for themselves of course, but to leave at the homes of poor or deprived children on the earth! They told us that they simply de-materialised the toys, took them away and re-materialised them where they felt they were most needed. So simple to them – but so effective – and so appreciated by the recipients I am sure.

Conversely we often received small gifts like wrapped toffees which were apported into the room and dropped on our knees in the darkness during the sitting. Most interestingly, on one of these occasions Sydney examined the wrappers and was intrigued to note that, from his knowledge of the confectionery trade, **these particular sweets were a brand not available in the Middlesbrough area!**

We were told at a later sitting that they had been apported from a large party in London and the few we had would not have been missed from the dozens of dishes around the room.

But the party on 5th January 1954 was a particularly memorable one in that a close friend of ours, Jim McKenzie, an electrical engineer, had arranged to record the whole sitting – and I still have a copy of that tape which 'Mac' played to hundreds of people at numerous public meetings in the North East.

And herein lies the story of The two Indian-style bells (Photo 'E').

I had the microphone and was giving a running commentary during the sitting.

As usual the first part was held in complete darkness for the trumpet phenomena and it was during this period that we all heard the tinkling of a small bell. The only bell in that room, which was our children's playroom in our own home, was a small Indian style bell which stood on the mantelpiece. Our children played with it regularly and had in fact broken one of the prongs. On hearing the ringing I immediately said that the Spirit children were obviously enjoying themselves and ringing our bell.

After a few moments the ringing stopped and there was a gentle 'plop' on the carpet. I remarked that they had finished with the bell and dropped it on the carpet. A few moments later however the ringing started again and I well remember saying that they had fooled me and picked it up again. This time the ringing lasted a little longer and again there was the 'plop' when it was dropped on to the carpet.

At the end of the sitting which lasted about one and a half hours we were all amazed when the room lights went on. **There on the carpet in the middle of the room lay not one – but two bells!**

Our own damaged bell was there, with a slightly larger one lying about two feet away from it. **This larger one was an *apport*.** Where I had assumed that they had picked up our bell, they had in fact brought into the sitting this second one, and had certainly fooled me – but not in the way I had thought at the time!

When we checked the tone of each bell there was a slight difference but my untrained ear had failed to notice this during the sitting. It was, of course, very interesting to listen to the recording when we played it back during our supper after the sitting. The difference could be heard but it is so slight that I am not surprised I had been fooled.

I still have both these bells kept together in my box of memorabilia. The surface of our original one with the broken prong has gradually tarnished – as would be expected. **But not so with the apported bell which has retained its new-looking shine and looks no different from the day we received it over 30 years ago.**

It may be that the metal surfaces were treated in different ways during manufacture – which I don't know of course – but I find it rather intriguing, to say the least.

MY PRAYER

(Composed and dictated by Aunt Agg when she materialised at our sitting on 21st July 1953, especially for the benefit of Mr Brittain Jones – as explained after the poem.)

In the long and silent watches of the dark and dreary night.
My soul cries out in anguish to the God of Love and Light.

Send down Thy Holy Angels in this my darkest hour,
That they may give me Light and Hope and give my Soul the power
To rise above the sordidness of earthly cares and strife,
That I may look to brighter things in that Eternal Life –

Where Love is crowned with happiness, where all is fair and bright,
Where flowers bloom with sweet perfume and where there is no night.

My Soul arises unafraid, my night of sorrow o'er,
Oh God of Love ,Thou leadest me towards that Heavenly shore.

My heart cries out with thanks to Thee for all Thy loving care
Into Thy hands Oh Lord I come – Thou answerest now MY PRAYER.

A FEW weeks previously Mr Jones had been talking to *Aunt Agg* about his personal feelings. He had told her there were many times when he felt that life on earth held little interest for him now. He had been used to an extremely busy life but his medical activities had ceased many years ago. This frustration caused by his inactivity and failing health meant that his still very alert mind was constantly seeking answers to his ever-present problem – especially at night when he was unable to sleep.

He commented that his usefulness here was finished and he was looking forward to joining her and his many friends in the Spirit world to "start a new life". *Aunt Agg* in her inimitable quiet manner explained to him that he would join them when the time was right and his Spirit was ready to make the transition. She added that patience was truly a virtue, and as he readily agreed it was never one of his strong points. Now was the time for him to try to understand and learn.

He said he would try his best not to get too depressed and *Aunt Agg* promised they would help him as much as possible – but there was still much he himself needed to do. We must live our own lives to form our own individual characters and they were always ready to help and guide us in times of need – but the final decisions were always in our own hands.

It was a few weeks after this conversation that *Aunt Agg* materialised as usual, sat down on a chair in front of the cabinet curtain and dictated this poem. In the fairly bright red light I was able to write it down as she dictated it. She told Mr Jones it was specially for him, hoped it would help him and felt that it probably epitomised his feelings at those certain times which she had shared with him in his home on a number of occasions since their conversation.

He was most grateful and thanked her very much. I gave him a typed copy a few days later and I am sure it did help him. He became a much more relaxed and calmer man during the few months before he joined his friends in the Spirit world later that year aged 76 years.

APPORTS; TELEKINESIS; SPIRIT WRITING; SPIRIT LIGHTS

MY notebooks show that from our second sitting on 27th April 1946, we had regular evidence of these types of phenomena. Hardly a Saturday passed without some brief reference to them. In the first six months we had received over 60 apports and there were numerous instances of the other types of phenomena. Detailed lists can be very boring so here are just a few of those early happenings which not only amazed and pleased us, but made us realise that we were entering an entirely 'new world' of **Physical Phenomena** as far as we were all concerned. It was exciting and thrilling, but we were never self-deceptive and always 'kept our feet firmly on the ground'.

APPORTS *(from the French 'apporter' — to bring).*

These are normal material things which are either brought into or taken out of the Circle room without human contact. We understand from our Spirit helpers that they usually de-materialise the article, bring it 'through' the structure of the room and then re-materialise it in the room. Occasionally they would dematerialise the wall or woodwork and bring in the article as it was. Such apported articles remained in the room after the sitting finished and should not be confused with ectoplasmic materialisations which were in the room only during the period of sitting whilst the ectoplasm was emanating from the medium.

Amongst those early apports were – a Canadian five cent piece, 1889; an old penny from a box of coins I kept at home; a pair of cuff-links from the home of one of the sitters; many flowers including *a sprig of white blossom (our very first apport during our third sitting)*, lily of the valley, roses, tulips, carnations, asters, chrysanthemums, marguerites, dahlias, gaillardia and others.

But there were **two particularly interesting apports** in those early days –

• At that time, immediately after the end of the war, luminous paint was just not obtainable. I remembered that I had had an old wrist watch with luminous figures on the face which I thought might still be in a drawer at my parents' house. Mam spent quite a lot of time searching, but told us before our ninth sitting on 29th June that she had been unsuccessful. Imagine our amazement when we put on the room light at the end of the sitting, **there on the top of the clock** on the mantelpiece **was my watch**. Our Spirit friends had obviously known exactly where it was.

• At the end of the eleventh sitting there, lying on the hearth, was a cutting from a type of scented bush called Southernwood. Mrs Hildred could hardly believe it. Only three hours earlier she had been at home talking to her sister and said she wanted a piece for transplanting. *Sam Hildred* told us he had overheard the conversation and **thought he'd save her the trouble**!

Later, the fully materialised Spirit people often brought apports and handed them personally to the thrilled recipients. Over the years we had many hundreds of **apports** of various kinds.

TELEKINESIS *(Movement of material objects without human contact)*

Each week the **trumpet**, which was standing on a wooden board in the centre of the Circle, tapped in time to our singing. An **ashtray** was moved from the mantelpiece to elsewhere in the room and many times the things on the mantelpiece were shifted around without our knowing it during the sitting. We only saw the changes when the light went on at the end of the sitting. A **1⅓lb. brass bell** in the form of a crinoline lady which Syd and Gladys kept on the mantelpiece (as seen in photos 'B' & 'C') was frequently rung during the sittings by our Spirit visitors.

During the tenth sitting Sam Hildred removed his photograph from the mantelpiece and placed it gently on Gladys' knee – all in complete darkness without any human contact.

SPIRIT WRITING

We generally put a piece of paper on the fireplace hearth, together with a pencil – always hoping that some Spirit friend may be able to 'sign in'. We were delighted that at the end of the seventeenth sitting **we found a number of signatures on it** – Jack – Agnes – Mona (Gladys's sister in Spirit) – Ivy (Doris's sister in Spirit) and a rough circle which we understood was *Sunrise's* sign. *I still have that sheet of paper with the signatures on it and more followed in later weeks.*

Sam Hildred was always a joker and decided to be different. He told us, through the trumpet, that he had signed his name but we would have to look for it. After the light went on at the end of the sitting it took us some considerable time before we finally found it – **written on a tile on the front of the tiled fireplace**, down at the bottom right hand corner!

One other most intriguing piece of writing a few weeks later simply said – **"Not blind now"**. We made enquiries from *Aunt Agg* the following week and were told it had been written by a very dear friend of my Mam and Dad, *Mr Cowell Pugh*. He had passed over many years previously – but **when living on the earth he had become totally blind**. He was always a bright and forceful personality and was obviously no different in the Spirit world – **except that he was 'not blind now'!**

SPIRIT LIGHTS

My notes for sitting No 26 on 26th October 1946 show that we had four **Spirit lights** at about one minute intervals, each lasting for two or three seconds, before the trumpet phenomena began. They were about one inch in diameter and appeared in the area in front of the fireplace.

As we developed, we had many more instances of such type of lights much brighter than the first four. Often two or three would be seen at the same time and they would remain for eight or nine seconds. **We were told that they were in fact the incandescent ends of ectoplasmic rods which were emanating from the medium.**

About a year later, on the 22nd November 1947, we were startled by a number of **very bright flashes of Spirit lights** – completely different from the earlier type which had ceased some months ago. Each flash **lit up the whole room**, very similar to a camera flashgun – but I can assure you there was no such equipment in that room.

A few came before the trumpet phenomena with more coming from behind the cabinet curtain during the materialisation. They were of such intensity that even with only the 15 inch gap at the top the entire room was illuminated. We were told that *Gladys's brother in Spirit, Douglas, was the 'technician' responsible for these particular Spirit lights.*

Four weeks later on 20th December, as *Aunt Agg* was drawing back the cabinet curtain to step into the room for her weekly chat, her face was lit up by two bright lights from behind the curtain. From this you will understand that **these lights were under the complete control of our Spirit helpers and therefore not dangerous to the medium** – unlike any unexpected bright light used by anyone sitting in the Circle, which is extremely dangerous.

As I have said, these are but a very few instances of the regular weekly happenings we were so privileged to witness. I trust you have found them interesting and perhaps thought provoking.

*   *   *   *

(More poems found in my mother's papers after her passing to the Spirit world).

No funeral gloom my dears, When I am gone;
Corpse-gazing; tears; black raiment; graveyard grimness;
Think of me as withdrawn into the dimness, –
Yours still – you mine; remember all the best
Of our past moments – and forget the rest.

Cremate my body then my dears. When I am gone;
Think of my soul in realms supernal,
Returning oft to earth from the Eternal;
Yours still – you mine; united still in love
Till God shall call you too my dears – above.

*   *   *   *

There's never a night goes by but someone's saying a prayer
That the one they dearly love will be helped their pain to bear;
That the morning will bring strength, and hope dispel all fears;
This prayer is being said tonight by a thousand hearts in tears.

There's never a morning breaks but some of our hopes come true;
Maybe it's turned out this way for the one you love – and you.
But remember those who still weep and whose prayers have seemed in vain.
Then out of your thankful heart say the prayer you prayed – again.

HEALING ASPECTS

OUR Saturday night Home Circle was always a Healing Centre for those in need and its value as such was illustrated in so many ways for so many different people. Perhaps one of the more significant aspects was the healing given to my mother, our medium. I was frequently asked, whether the physical phenomena had any ill-effect on the medium's health. I was delighted to assure them that certainly in my mother's case the reverse was in fact true.

Mother had her first operation for breast cancer in 1942 and by the time we started our Home Circle in April 1946 the use of her left arm was seriously impaired by the swollen lymphatic glands. There was a constant nagging pain and she was unable to raise the arm above waist high – but her inherent cheerfulness and resolution kept it all very low profile.

By the mid-1950s we had been sitting for 7 to 8 years and she had been operated upon numerous times. Each time the consulting surgeon commented on her remarkable powers of recuperation and on one particular occasion added, with some apparent bewilderment, "Someone else seems to be doing you more good than we are!" Little did he know the real truth of his comments. Fortunately, today's medical profession is not so bigoted and many doctors are not averse to recommending 'alternative medicine', including Spirit healing.

One particularly intriguing aspect of the healing given to mother during our sittings was demonstrated to us when Sunrise was controlling her – usually at the end of the trumpet voice phenomena – before she moved on to the chair behind the cabinet curtain ready for the materialisation phenomena.

Sunrise would stand her up and then tell us he would help the medium's arm. With no more ado he would immediately raise mother's left arm vertically above her head – something she had been unable to do for many years – and then start swinging it round and round like a propeller. After three or four minutes of this rapid exercise he would bring the arm to rest down by her side, stand for a moment or two and then walk her the few steps to the chair in the cabinet and sit her down.

Mam, being in deep trance, was completely unaware of this arm-swinging, the same as she was unaware of all the physical phenomena that occurred – but we always told her about it while having our cup of tea afterwards. She was always amazed and try as hard as she could was never able to raise it above her waist.

Mam's normal sleep pattern was very irregular because of the ever-present nagging pains, but after our sittings on Saturday evenings she always enjoyed four to five hours solid sleep that night. **If the physical phenomena took any energy out of her – as some people seem to think – then her Spirit guides and healers replaced it – with added beneficial effects.**

In addition to our Saturday evening sittings, we also held a Healing Circle in our own home during the week. Mother often attended, purely as a patient, and received further healing from another of our members, a staunch friend, Mr Wilf Waite.

We were told that, in general, the same team of Spirit helpers was at both Circles and it was encouraging to know that the power needed to heal others was closely linked with the power we gave for the physical phenomena on Saturday evenings. **In effect – the more we gave – the more we received – the more to be able to help others!**

AN ECTOPLASMIC FEATHER FROM SUNRISE

A S previously explained, **ectoplasm** is a material produced by the Spirit chemists, which emanates from the medium's body and **is at all times connected to the medium.**

This is extremely important and any experiments involving ectoplasm **must** have the approval of the Spirit helpers. Their co-operation is essential, otherwise the medium could be in great danger.

After Mr Jones had satisfied his medical interest by taking the pulse of *Aunt Agg's* materialised body in December 1946, we asked *Aunt Agg* **whether it might be possible to have a specimen piece of ectoplasm** – perhaps by cutting a piece from her robes which always clothed her body. (See Photograph 'B').

She told us it should be all right but would let us know later when everything had been arranged to protect 'our Min', as she always called her sister, the medium. This experiment was actually carried out on two occasions in May 1947 *(see 'Pieces of Ectoplasm cut from Aunt Agg's Robes')* – but a month earlier, in April, Sunrise had told us he would materialise and bring with him an **ectoplasmic feather**.

He asked that we should have a suitable sized jar with a little water in the bottom ready for the feather – so, in case of accidents, we actually had two slightly different sized jars each with a screw-on lid and a little water in the bottom. They were placed on the mantelpiece ready for use during the sitting.

That evening, 26th April, we had some excellent trumpet voice phenomena, including *Sam Hildred* who stayed for almost 10 minutes chatting in his own inimitable style. His widow was now a regular sitter with us and she never had any doubts that the Spirit person she heard and regularly conversed with was her husband – and he seldom missed a week, even if it was for only a few moments.

On this particular evening he told her he had brought her five carnations which she would find in the room at the close of the sitting, as a present for their Wedding Anniversary that weekend – and they were certainly there as he had promised!

After the trumpet phenomena, our materialisation phenomena followed in the usual red light, which by now was bright enough to see the materialised forms quite distinctly. Mother's mediumship had developed considerably over the 12 months.

After two Spirit people had materialised and spoken to us, *Sunrise* then spoke to us from behind the cabinet curtain using Direct Voice i.e. using an ectoplasmic voice box but without the trumpet. He said he was going to 'build', but as he had never done this before it would take a lot of power and *Aunt Agg* would come immediately after him to bring the feather he had promised.

He also said that there was not quite enough liquid in the jars but not to bother as the Spirit chemists would attend to that!

Within two or three minutes the curtain was drawn back by this **tallish figure complete with a full feathered head-dress!** He stayed for about two minutes and then stepped back behind the curtain – a very moving experience for all of us to actually meet our Circle leader on the Spirit side face to face.

Within another couple of minutes *Aunt Agg* stepped forward from the cabinet in her usual friendly manner. We clearly saw that she was holding not one feather, but

two feathers. She explained that **one of them was an apport** i.e. a material feather from somewhere outside the Circle room, and she placed it on the mantelpiece alongside her. **The other one was made of ectoplasm** and she handed it to my father, who always sat next to the cabinet, and asked him to pass it round the sitters.

We were all bubbling with excitement but did not allow this to overcome our usual 'investigative' outlook. We carefully felt the texture and generally agreed that it felt very similar to the wing feather of a medium sized bird – quite firm and springy – and was about three inches long.

I was the last to examine it, at the other end of the Circle. I then handed it back to Doris to hand to *Aunt Agg* who had been standing in the middle of the room watching us while the feather was being passed around. But instead of *Aunt Agg* taking it, she simply moved over to the fireplace, picked up one of the jars and asked Doris to drop the feather in. *Aunt Agg* then picked up the lid from the mantelpiece and screwed it on the jar – in full view of all the sitters.

Aunt Agg stayed for a while chatting and we thanked her for such a remarkable and enjoyable 12 months. She replied by saying that the Spirit helpers, including herself, were all astounded by the amazing progress that had been made in such a short time. They would always be willing to help us with our interesting 'experiments', but asked us to always remember the original purpose of our Home Circle – regular meetings with friends and relatives from the Spirit world. We assured them that we would never forsake that most important aspect of our sittings.

Just before we closed, Sunrise again spoke to us by Direct Voice and told us we would be able to cut a piece from Aunt Agg's robes within the next few weeks, for which we thanked him very much.

MORE INFORMATION ABOUT THE TWO FEATHERS

(a) **The Apport Feather** - which had been placed on the mantelpiece by *Aunt Agg*. This was about five inches long, bright reddish-orange in colour and much softer than the Ectoplasmic feather we had all handled during the sitting. We don't know where it actually came from, but **I still have it in my possession** *(See Photograph 'D')*.

(b) **The Ectoplasmic Feather – in the jar with the lid on**. The first thing we noticed was that there was **at least one inch of liquid in the jar**, whereas the other jar had the same shallow covering of the bottom as when we started. The **Spirit chemists had added more liquid** just as *Sunrise* had intimated before he materialised.

The jar was passed round and we all examined the contents closely – especially my mother who had no idea what had been happening while she had been in deep trance. Sydney had a watch repairer's magnifying eye-glass and we all used it to have an even closer examination of the feather, and I quote from my recorded notes which I made that evening –

"It was white and looked like plastic – certainly a very different texture from the coloured apport feather on the mantelshelf. Sunrise had told us that it would soon disappear and in fact we were able to watch that actually happen in front of our eyes during supper. It seemed to gradually melt away into little drops of fluid and run into the bottom of the jar. We removed the lid after about an hour and a

quarter (the feather had been put in about 9.00 pm.) and we could smell a kind of bleach/chlorine odour. By 11.30 pm. the feather had completely gone and only fluid was left in the jar."

Mr Jones took about half the fluid to analyse in his hospital laboratory – anticipating to discover something unusual – but no such thing. He told us the following week that the crystals he obtained from his centrifuge showed nothing unusual and the major constituents were akin to the chemicals used in bleaching agents – as the odour from the jar had indicated.

Irrespective of that slight anti-climax to our investigative outlook, we were still delighted to have had the unique opportunity of **retaining,** even for only a short period, a specimen of **ectoplasm after the sitting had closed.** And we were keenly anticipating the promised experiment in a few weeks time.

PIECES OF ECTOPLASM CUT FROM
AUNT AGG'S ROBES

A T the close of our fifty-second sitting on 26th April 1947, during which we had received the ectoplasmic feather, *Sunrise* had promised us that within a few weeks we would have the opportunity of cutting a piece of ectoplasm from *Aunt Agg's* robes. True to his promise, three weeks later, *Aunt Agg* spoke to Mr Jones and asked him to have his scissors ready for the following week.

Usually *Granny Lumsden* was the first to materialise each week, but this particular week, 24th May, *Aunt Agg* came first. She came out from the cabinet, stood in front of Mr Jones and invited him to cut off a piece of her ectoplasmic robes which she held up towards him. As he cut off a piece about the size of a small pocket handkerchief we all saw *Aunt Agg* cringe a little and heard a slight gasp from my mother behind the cabinet curtain.

Being an experiment approved by our Spirit helpers my mother suffered no ill effect; but here again I can only emphasise the importance of such approval in relation to the safety of the medium. **Materialisation mediums in deep trance place their trust in the hands of the sitters and that trust is sacrosanct!**

The piece of ectoplasm was passed around the sitters and then I placed it on the mantelpiece alongside me. After *Aunt Agg* went, *Sunrise* spoke to us and said that they too were experimenting this week and did not expect the ectoplasm to be still there when the Circle closed.

He asked us not to be too disappointed however, as we would be able to repeat the experiment next week, when we should have another small jar ready to receive it – as we had done with the ectoplasmic feather. **But this time, he said, just provide the empty jar and the Spirit chemists would put in some liquid to try to keep the ectoplasm a little longer.**

After a number of other materialisations we closed at 9.20 pm. and as expected, when the room lights went on there was no ectoplasm to be seen. But we were all looking forward to the following week of course!

The following week, 31st May, it happened that we had previously arranged to have two guest visitors – a Chartered Accountant friend of Sydney's and the Matron of a large local hospital who had worked with Mr Jones for many years. We asked *Sunrise* if we ought to re-arrange their visit but it was agreed we should go ahead as usual – much to our visitors' delight when we explained to them before we started.

We had our usual excellent trumpet voice phenomena and some flower apports were given to our visitors, including a rose and two carnations. After about half an hour my mother went into the cabinet and our materialisation phenomena followed. Firstly there was a close nursing colleague from the same hospital as Mr Jones and the Matron, followed by the accountant's mother.

In both cases the visitors were quite certain of the identity of the materialised spirits and were extremely thrilled and happy to be able to meet and talk to them again.

Then *Aunt Agg* came, and after chatting to our visitors in her usual friendly manner, she turned to Mr Jones to repeat last week's cutting. The piece of ectoplasm was again passed round the sitters, including our visitors, and then I unscrewed the lid of the jar, which had been standing on the mantelpiece all evening, put in the ectoplasm and screwed on the lid.

At no other time was the lid not screwed on the jar, but as I put in the ectoplasm I was aware of the same 'bleach-like' odour as the jar with the ectoplasmic feather some five weeks earlier. I was also able to see sufficiently in the dim red light, **that the jar was about one third full of liquid – again supplied by the Spirit chemists as** *Sunrise* **had said.** Another remarkable apport.

When the room lights went on at the close of the sitting the piece of ectoplasm was still there in the liquid in the jar. Again we all examined it very closely, especially my mother of course, and agreed it looked like very, very fine cotton material, with one of the ladies commenting that it reminded her of 'chiffon' – a gossamer-like material.

Naturally we were very excited to have been privileged to carry out such a unique experiment – especially in the presence of our two visitors who were so thrilled to have been part of it.

By the time we left Syd and Gladys's the ectoplasm was still in the jar and had dissolved only very slightly – quite different from the ectoplasmic feather which completely dissolved into the liquid within two and a half hours.

The jar was left on the mantelpiece and the ectoplasm gradually dissolved over the next four days until by the following Wednesday there was only the yellowish liquid with a few minute specks suspended therein.

I have never heard of such an experiment being carried out in any other Home Circle or séance, but would be delighted to hear from any reader who has been as privileged as we were – and who perhaps was able to obtain more 'scientific' information.

*   *   *   *

In the last analysis, it is our conception of death which decides our answers to all the questions that life puts to us.

Dag Hammarskjold

A MOST UNUSUAL APPORT AND BIRTHDAY GIFT

ONE of the most unusual and certainly the largest apport received through my mother's mediumship occurred not in a Home Circle sitting, but in my mother's home on her 53rd birthday – 17th March 1948.

Mam and Dad had a fish and chip shop in Middlesbrough and lived behind the shop. The kitchen had a small 'walk-in' type of pantry with no window, only a zinc-gauze vent, which was the norm in those days in the North East. It was in here that this exceptional apport occurred.

Doris and I lived about 10 minutes drive from the shop and about four o'clock our telephone rang. It was Mam asking me if I could go straight there as there was something unusual she wanted me to see. As I helped in the shop each morning I thought it was probably something to do with the business – but nothing more was said, and I left immediately.

When I arrived Mam and Dad were sitting in the kitchen having a cup of tea. Mam usually had a smile on her face, but on this occasion it seemed rather enigmatic. She realised I was keen to see what she had telephoned about and immediately said –

"Just open the pantry door, son, but be very careful."

Naturally I was very curious and not a little apprehensive – but did exactly as I was asked. I opened it very slowly but because of the lack of light saw nothing unusual for a moment or two. Then as I opened it wider to step inside I was halted in my tracks!

There at my feet on the floor of the pantry was a mass of lilac blossom* – filling the whole floor space and as high as the first shelf – about three feet high!

I turned and looked at Mam who, with an even bigger grin, said *"I thought you'd be surprised"*, an understatement if ever there was. But the explanation was even more surprising.

Mam had made the customary pot of tea in the afternoon, got the milk jug out of the pantry, closed the door behind her and sat on her chair adjacent to the door. She then realised that she had forgotten the sugar, turned on her chair and opened the door again – to be confronted by this amazing sight on the pantry floor.

One moment earlier, when she got the milk, the floor had been absolutely clear. Now it was packed with lilac blossom. Naturally they were both dumbfounded and Mam's first thought was to ring me. I was as amazed as they were.

Instinctively I knew it was not a practical joke. Mam and Dad didn't do those things, and Mam wouldn't bring me back to the shop 'on a fool's errand'.

It had certainly happened as Mam said. There was no doubt about that. A few other instances of individual flower apports had occurred outside the Circle room, but usually during the time we were actually sitting. This mass of lilac blossom however was quite exceptional and Mam was clearly non-plussed but very excited.

Needless to say we immediately removed it, made it up into a number of bunches and I took them round to many of our delighted friends where they lasted two or three weeks – as normal.   *(*Lilac doesn't bloom in Middlesbrough in March!)*

Come the following Saturday evening, *Aunt Agg* again pre-empted our question by asking us to tell 'our Min', that they had been delighted to be able to bring her such a special birthday gift from her many Spirit friends who were so close to her!

The darkness of the pantry had afforded the ideal conditions and it was another example of Mam's remarkable mediumship. But for a change, this time she had been the first to witness it!

THE MISSING POUND NOTE

B Y 1950 Doris and I were living in a terraced house in Oxford Road, Middlesbrough. We then had a family of five children with ages ranging from three to nine years, and had little money to spare. Doris in fact had become very adept at making a little go a very long way.

She always folded the few pound notes individually in her purse and always knew how many she had. When at home, she left her purse on a high shelf on the Welsh dresser in the living room. I came home one evening to find her very upset because she was fairly certain that a pound note was missing from her purse.

She had questioned all the children and they had assured her that they were not involved. Doubts of all kinds pass through parents' minds at times like this, but we had no reason not to believe them – and left it at that.

Naturally we were still concerned that we had lost about one sixth of our weekly income – and still rather puzzled. Doris checked and rechecked her spending and was still fairly certain that a pound was missing – but we said nothing to anyone else.

Come the following Sunday evening however we had a most unexpected and pleasant surprise – although by now, after four years of the remarkable phenomena in our Home Circle, we should not have been so surprised. But this occasion was slightly different and was not during one of our sittings.

Mam and Dad used to visit us for tea most Sundays and stay to watch the regular weekly play on television. There was always an interval during the play (e.g. the potter's wheel; the playful kitten; etc.) when Doris would make the usual cup of tea. On this particular Sunday, Doris popped into the kitchen and I was sitting next to Mam, ready to have a little chat.

Before I could say anything however, within 30 seconds she was in trance, eyes closed, and *Aunt Agg* was speaking to us. The sisters had such a close psychic rapport that it was as simple as that.

She immediately told me that she was fully aware of our concern about the missing pound note and firstly assured us that none of our children was involved. I called Doris back from the kitchen and *Aunt Agg* then proceeded to tell us what had actually happened.

Because of the strength of the psychic power in our house, Spirit people could easily use it to move things around, as we had often noticed. Harmless fun by the Spirit children which we never discouraged and usually had a good laugh about. But on this occasion things were different.

This time it was a young boy, recently passed over, who had not been averse to 'nicking' the odd item when on the earth and his outlook had not had time to change since his passing. This is quite normal and poltergeists are an extreme example of this inability to understand their change of state – from earthly to Spirit beings.

He had taken the note from Doris's purse with the intention of keeping it but because of the protective 'psychic aura' provided by our close Spirit helpers, he found he could not take it out of the house and had therefore just left it. *Aunt Agg* then told us he had actually left it under the refrigerator in the kitchen – probably thinking he was hiding it and would not be 'found out'.

I thanked *Aunt Agg* very much indeed and said I would immediately retrieve it. She said she would wait until we had actually recovered it and had been only too pleased to be able to help – especially to clear the bairns, as she called them.

Sure enough, by raking under the one inch gap below the fridge with a long garden cane, THE POUND NOTE CAME OUT – along with much dust and fluff of course! And it was still folded in Doris's usual way. *Aunt Agg* then chuckled in her inimitable way, said 'Cheerio' and within another 30 seconds mother came out of her trance, when we were able to tell her what had happened.

Just another example of the closeness of our Spirit friends who are always amongst us and show their caring when it is needed. They are still part of our family and act in the same way that families do – by helping whenever possible. But they do not interfere and run our lives for us – that is always our own personal responsibility.

We still had time for our cup of tea before the end of the 15 minute interval, and we were then able to tell Mam all about it. Remember, she knew nothing about the affair until we told her after *Aunt Agg* had gone and she was just as pleased as we were to hear of the 'happy ending'.

THE BOUNDLESS UNIVERSE

The Sun is so large that it could contain more than 1,000,000 worlds the size of our **Earth**.

There are **Stars** so large that they could easily contain 500,000,000 **Suns**.

There are 100,000,000,000 **Stars** in the average **Galaxy**, with 100,000,000 **Galaxies in known Space!**

WHAT THEN OF THE UNKNOWN?

*　　　　*　　　　*　　　　*

"And ever near us though unseen. Our Dear Immortal Spirits tread,
For all the Boundless Universe is life – There are no dead."

A LETTER – FORTY YEARS ON

DURING one of his occasional calls at my home in late 1988, I mentioned to one of my brothers-in-law, Tony Carr, that I was writing a book about our Home Circle. My notebook showed that he had been a guest at sitting No.97 on 28th February 1948, when he was a rather sceptical young man in his early twenties. Tony now has a B.A. degree and has spent his working life in the scientific and technical fields allied to the motor industry. He is Managing Director of his own successful medium-sized company and is meticulous in his attention to detail.

He recounted to me his still vivid memories of his visit to our Circle and later wrote me a letter, from which I would now like to quote –

I hadn't realised Tom, that you had kept a diary of your Circle meetings and found it very interesting but also shattering that it was some 40 years ago! Some of the things I had forgotten, but there were two other factors not mentioned by you which I believe are worth recording.

Firstly – before it began Syd advised me to check the whole room to ensure that the only means of access was the door; that the window was closed and blacked out and could not be opened from the outside; and to make sure there were no trap-doors in the floor or ceiling! I can still remember him saying 'People will tell you there were ways of entry into the room. Oh, they will you know!' I must admit I was reluctant to do so but I did it to satisfy Syd, and needless to say, once the door was closed there was no means of entry.

Secondly – the materialised form of my relative had quite a strong beard and he insisted that I pulled it hard to prove it was not false. I did and there was no way I could detach it from his face! It didn't occur to me at the time that my actions might have caused him some pain – the vigour of my pull would certainly have caused you or I to yell out. But there was no reaction from him.

But to me the most significant part of the evening was the trumpet movement prior to the commencement of the Spirit voices. The members of the Circle sat around the trumpet and relatively near to it. In such a small room it was impossible for anyone to move without some of the remaining members being aware of such movement.

I vividly recall the trumpet slowly rising from the floor (the fluorescent paint on it gave a slight glow in the dark and therefore 'positioned' it for us) and beginning to move around the Circle. It moved up and down in front of each of us, going faster and faster but without ever touching either the floor or our feet. Then it would move up to the ceiling again, never ever touching it.

There was no possible way that any sitter could move that physical object so rapidly and diversely IN THE DARK. As you know Tom, I have spent my working life in the scientific and technical fields and this event remains as the one outstanding experience for which I cannot find, or even imagine, an explanation in physical terms.

Wouldn't it be good if we could experience these things again or at least share them even more fully with others.

Yes, Tony, it certainly would be – and I only hope this book will go some way along that road for the benefit of others.

LOOKING FORWARD

(Another poem found in my mother's papers after her passing in 1958)

Take the road that stretches out before you,
Walk in the dusk and know the end is bright.
Take what comes and find the way to glory,
Much may go wrong – but even more comes right.

Face the day however hard before you
And with the tears upon your cheek still wet,
Learn to smile and keep on looking forward –
Life is not done because the Sun is set!

A T the end of my illustrated talks in the 1960s and 70s I always invited questions and comments from the audience. Lively discussions generally ensued and the idea of this book was born; but for various reasons the actual 'birth' has been delayed.

Unfortunately there can be no such 'open session' at the end of a book, but I feel sure that for those seriously-minded readers wishing to investigate further, there will always be someone or some reliable and helpful organisation not too far away. 'Seek and ye shall find' is as applicable as ever it was and you could be pleasantly surprised by what might be 'in your own back yard'.

What was witnessed in our Home Circle was undeniable *proof to those present;* but it can never be proof to anyone else – and I would never suggest it should be.

For you it can be nothing more than evidence – the strength of which is commensurate with the credibility of its source; as with the jury in a Court of Law. I trust I have impressed you as a genuine and honest witness – I have no reason whatsoever to be otherwise – but you must make the final judgment.

Accept only what appeals to your reasoning and level of understanding, bearing in mind how our perception changes wish increased knowledge. Scientists today are regularly disproving yesterday's 'facts'. What is 'true' today is so often replaced by another 'truth' tomorrow. Keep an open mind at all times and be ready to seize your piece of personal proof when it presents itself – quite likely from a most unexpected or unpredictable source.

Be sure that you are ready for that propitious moment when it presents itself. But don't be expecting a 'world shattering' experience. It will most likely be a simple but very meaningful happening unique to yourself – a moment of indefinable enlightenment – an unforgettable moment to be forever treasured.

Thank you sincerely for your company on this very brief sojourn down Memory Lane; Even though you may never have the thrill and privilege of meeting your Spirit loved ones face to face – very few ever do – **always remember that they are around and amongst us,** ever ready to make their presence felt whenever the opportunity arises.

It is an old maxim of mine that when you have excluded the impossible, whatever remains, however improbable, **Must be the Truth.**   *Sir Arthur Conan Doyle.*

LIFE ON THE OTHER SIDE

SINCE the publication of this book in 1989, I have frequently been asked if the Spirit visitors to our Home Circle ever described what life is like in the Spirit world – that is on the 'Other Side' and the simple answer is 'Yes', on many occasions.

With the benefit of hindsight, I now realise that I should have included a brief article on this aspect in the book but with having to select just a few of so very many remarkable experiences of the actual Physical Phenomena, which I thought would be more interesting, I completely overlooked something which is obviously as interesting as the phenomena to so many people. In this edition I will now try to redress my omission.

Aunt Agg (Mrs. Agnes Abbott) was our main source of such information, although *Sam Hildred, Mona Hildred, Uncle Jack (Bessant)* and others also talked occasionally about their life in the Spirit world. They all emphasised that their world and life therein is just as real as this physical life.

The mind which controls the spirit body is exactly the same as that which controlled the physical body, and thus retains the character, memory, emotion, affection etc. etc. We do not suddenly change when we lose this physical body.

At first, individuals still retain their convictions and feelings about various subjects and still have the same outlook as they did immediately before their passing to the Spirit world. We certainly do not become 'goody-goody angels' or the fount of all knowledge. Not at all. Our development as an individual continues in a manner similar to that on earth but it is governed more by our conduct to our fellow spirit beings; with superficial values of material wealth, financial power or social importance, etc. vanishing when the physical body is discarded and we do not have the day to day problems of having to 'earn a living' to clothe, house and maintain that body.

Some people who do not believe in a continuing existence in a Spirit world find it extremely difficult to come to terms with their new life and sometimes cannot accept, or even want to accept that they have left their physical bodies. The reasons for such a confused state can be various but are often found in bigoted religious upbringing or in the kind of discreditable or wretched lives they have led on Earth. These latter, who are steeped in a 'materialistic outlook often still want to continue in the same way, causing trouble and chaos and they have a very difficult 'learning process' to go through before such problems arc eradicated.

We had a particularly interesting example, in our Home Circle, of an old neighbour who passed over through a heart attack at the bus stop one morning. Because of his religious beliefs he did not believe he was 'dead' and was completely puzzled why his daughters ignored him when he went into their home. He told a mutual friend, *Jack G.*, who had passed over shortly after this neighbour, that he couldn't be dead because he could see and talk to him (*Jack*). It took almost a year in our time before *Jack G.* was pleased to speak to us one evening and confirm that the neighbour had finally accepted that he had left his physical body and was now living in the Spirit world !

But such cases are the exception and the majority of people quickly adjust to their new environment, thoroughly enjoying a life unhindered by the dross of a physical body – especially where that body has become a useless shell, racked with disease causing untold pain. More importantly, not one of them ever said that they wanted to come back here. Quite the reverse in fact. They were adamant that life in the Spirit world was so much better and they were patiently waiting for the time when their loved ones would rejoin them.

However, as *Aunt Agg* often reminded us – as good as life was in the Spirit world, we must live our lives here on Earth to the best of our abilities, learning the lessons which would help us over there, when it was our time to go – but not before. Suicide cases needed so much help and guidance, she said and often thanked us for the way we were able to assist them during our sittings.

I well remember during one of my mother's trance sittings, an elderly lady-spirit visitor, who had no knowledge of Spiritualism, was having great difficulty in 'controlling' the medium (that is speaking through the medium) but with the help and encouragement of her grandson, who was sitting with us in the Circle, she finally, managed to speak with great apprehension. Her first words, in a croaky voice, were, "Am I back on the Earth then?" hastily adding, immediately after our brief confirmation, "But I will be able to go back, won't I?" in very anxious voice. We assured her that she certainly could and would, at which her tone and demeanour quickly became much more relaxed. To be 'able to go back' had been of paramount importance to her; a strong indication that she preferred her life in the Spirit world.

It may seem strange to some readers but *Aunt Agg* would tell us that life there has many similarities to life here. The significant difference of course being the elimination of the need to provide all the material requirements for the physical body. There is no need to 'work' for remuneration to achieve such ends. This means that all our efforts may be directed towards those activities which interest us more and give us greater satisfaction.

The Spirit world is very much a counterpart of this world with spirits of all ages and levels of development. Children need to be nurtured and taught – not with the limited outlook of Earth, but of 'Life' overall. *Mona Hildred,* the daughter in the Spirit world of one of our Circle members, regularly spoke to her mother through the trumpet and told us how she had become the 'guardian' of a baby girl called *'Prudence'* in the Spirit world and always brought her to our Circle to join in and grow up with the other Spirit children who came each week. *Mona* passed over in 1933, when she was 12, so as she said to her Mam – she was a 'big girl' now (25 years in our time) and able to help other young children which she obviously enjoyed. *Ivy Hudson,* my first wife's sister, who passed over when she was a year old, about 20 years previously told us that she did similar work; along with many others.

Dedicated doctors and nurses can still pursue their 'calling' in the Spirit world in numerous ways. People who pass over after long and debilitating illnesses do not suddenly recover and become completely well again. Although they have lost the useless physical body, the spirit body and the mind are still in need of caring medical skills, often for some period of time, we are told. Large scale accidents and catastrophes need rescue teams from the spirit side, as well as from over here, to help both those who have passed over and those critically ill. The innumerable healers amid healing groups here are constantly in need of such valuable help.

Mona's brother, Douglas, who had passed to the Spirit world 30 years previously, as a baby, had become very interested in what he described as 'the spirit counterpart of electricity' and used to bring us Spirit lights of various kinds, including exceedingly bright flashes which lit up the whole room for 2 or 3 seconds. He told us in a sitting in August 1947 that he was also developing what he called 'Mind Pictures' to help those people who had just passed over to understand what had happened and where they were.

Now in 1993 I suppose we can compare *Douglas's* work with today's television and video recordings, so he was in advance of us.

Aunt Agg herself, who was a well known medium at the Marylebone Spiritualist Association (now SAGB.) before her passing, told us that there were times when she still operated as a medium in the Spirit world to contact spirit people who had progressed to another dimension and were unable to lower their vibrations to get in touch with friends and relatives who had just passed over. This may seem rather strange to some people here but it is no different from the way our mediums operate here on Earth to contact our Spirit friends just one step ahead of us.

As I have said, the Spirit world is just as real to them as the Earth is to us but on a different vibration. They have their 'Halls of Learning' covering any subject they wish, including art, music, philosophy, etc. Their gardens and countryside include plants and flowers of such bright but delicate colours that we cannot even visualise them - they are so different and have a special 'pristine' character. I feel sure that one of Arthur Findlay's books included similar reports through the mediumship of John Sloan and I am sure that readers will have come across such corroborative testimony in other books.

I do realise that it can be extremely difficult, if not almost impossible, for many people whose knowledge of spirit matters is very limited, to understand or accept that such a life of 'seeing and doing' came exist in a non-physical world. My simple reply is to remind those with this difficulty of the 'dream world' of our sleep state. There is certainly nothing physical about what we see and do in our dreams but I am sure you must agree that they can be just as REAL and often MORE VIVID than normal life. Analogies are never ideal but can often be helpful - which I trust this may be.

I hope this short addition will go some way to rectifying the omission from the original book concerning life in the Spirit world and that it may help to a greater understanding of what glorious pleasures lie head of us in 'Life on the Other Side'.

Tom Harrison.
December 1993.

41

EXTRACT FROM 'NEW LIGHT ON SURVIVAL'

by Roy Dixon Smith.

Roy Dixon-Smith was a Lt. Colonel in the Indian army and a man of some standing. While serving in India in 1934 he met Betty and her husband Stuart. After hearing of Stuart's death, in 1937, he made contact with Betty and in 1939 they were married. Their life together was very brief as Betty died of a heart disease in 1944. His quest for evidence of survival, through Spiritualism, then began. Having retired from the army he contacted the MSA in London in January 1945 where he was given impressive evidence via a psychometry reading; ~. the names of Betty and Ethel (Betty's real name- but never used).

From there he travelled far and wide in his search, sitting with many well-known mediums. He advertised in the 'Psychic News' for 'experience of genuine materialisation' and was so impressed with his experiences in our Circle that he included them in his book 'New Light on Survival', published in 1932.

ON the afternoon of 9th October (1948) I was met at the station by Mr Shipman. He took me in his car to his home where I found that a bedroom had been placed at my disposal, and I was entertained freely and most hospitably for the week-end.

They knew nothing whatever about me and had never heard of me (and vice-versa) until after my letter had appeared in the paper. The house was of the same general type as the one at Buckie, my host and his friends likewise business and professional people of the same outlook and social background. The circle whom I met that evening consisted of Mr and Mrs Shipman, the parents[1] of Mrs Shipman, Mrs Harrison the medium, who is an intimate friend of the Shipmans' and a short and somewhat plump middle-aged lady bearing not the least resemblance to Betty, her son and daughter-in-law, and a well known local doctor. I mention all these details to show how utterly preposterous and ridiculous would be any suggestion of fraud, even had it been possible to produce thereby the results described.

My letter in the *Psychic News* said that I wanted these experiences to include in a book, and thus that anyone who might give them to me would, in a way, probably be rendering a public service; and that is why they answered my plea, but they insisted, quite naturally, on my not disclosing their address to avoid being pestered by curiosity-mongers and others. For evidential reasons I revealed no details of my private life before the séance was over, and for the same reason they would have refused to have listened to them, since they were just as anxious as I for genuine evidence.

The room in which the séance was held is much the same as the one at Buckie[3] except that there is only one door, that being in the same relative position to the 'cabinet' and sitters as the window is in the Buckie house, while the mantelpiece is alongside and on the right of the corner that contained the cabinet. The cabinet in this case consisted of a single black curtain, which I helped to hang up myself across the corner of the room; it enclosed a space barely big enough to hold the medium on her chair. The light during the séance was a bright red electric light bulb in a bowl suspended from the centre of the ceiling. The room throughout the materialisations was thus brightly illuminated and the forms and their faces clearly seen. The circle of chairs was arranged close up to and blocking the door, and thus a little farther from the cabinet than at Buckie. The door was locked and the séance then commenced.

The first phase was 'direct voice' in the dark through a luminous-banded trumpet (better called megaphone) which darted about the room, sometimes high in the air, and often accompanying the singing like a conductor's baton. The trumpet hovered in front of the sitter to be addressed, and the voices came through, all being quite loud but some difficult to understand while others are perfectly clear. The circle guide, speaking through the trumpet, then gave an excellent description of Betty, remarking on her height, slimness, and beauty; all being facts unknown to anyone present except myself. Betty then attempted to speak to me; after prolonged and seemingly painful effort and a few exclamations to the effect that she couldn't do it, she managed to say, "I am your Betty."

During this phase, large pink carnations were apported into the room, one being dropped on each sitter's lap including mine. They were quite fresh. and moist as if with dew. There were no flowers of this type previously in the room or, so my host told me, anywhere else in the house. The medium all the while had been sitting with the rest of us in the circle and was not in trance.

At the close of this phase, which seemed to me to last about a quarter of an hour, the red light was switched on, the medium took her seat behind the curtain, and the materialisations commenced, of which there were about half a dozen in all.

I was introduced to each one of them in turn; all being deceased friends and close relatives of the sitters and thus thoroughly well known to them. I rose from my chair, walked up to them and shook them by the hand, and we made conventional remarks to each other just exactly as everyone does when first meeting a stranger. They were swathed in white muslin-like draperies and cowls that were the exact replicas of those worn by the forms in the Buckie séance. They were solid, natural and, except for their apparel, exactly like ordinary living people. In fact, had everyone been dressed similarly, it would have been quite impossible to distinguish these materialised forms from the rest of the company. Their hands felt perfectly natural and life-like in every respect and their handgrips were very firm. They smiled, laughed, and chatted to me and the others; all their features, complexions, and expressions being perfectly clear in that ample light. I repeat (and surely I cannot be more explicit) they were exactly like you or me in muslin draperies, and they behaved as we would behave if we dropped in amongst a circle of friends and relations plus one stranger for a few minutes' visit, and they were welcomed accordingly and just as naturally and unemotionally as we would be. There were mutual cheery good-byes as they departed, sinking apparently through the floor in precisely the same manner as the forms at Buckie.

My introduction to the first of them was "Come and meet Aunt Gladys[2]" (the sister of the medium), and she was most charming and vivacious as she offered me her hand and smiled and chatted to me. Then came 'Grannie', and as I was presented to her the doctor said to me "Feel her pulse". The old lady chuckled, extended her arm, made some humorous remark about 'mucking her about' or something to that effect, and I pressed my fingers into her wrist. All the sinews were there and the wrist felt and looked absolutely natural; the beat of the pulse was strong and regular.

"Now feel her feet," said the doctor, and I bent down and felt the foot that the laughing old lady extended from her long draperies. It felt rather spongy or woolly and was apparently about to dissolve, for just after that the old lady bade us farewell and vanished.

Then came a man with a twisted face drawn down rather grotesquely on the right side, as a consequence of which he could only mumble incoherently. I was introduced to him by name, and as I shook his hand my host explained, "He always comes like this. He died of a stroke".

I cannot remember the next two or three visitors very clearly, but what I have said of the others applies equally to them; and by then the slight feeling of oddity at this amazing experience had left me, for it was all so absolutely natural. They all differed drastically in face, figure, voice, and mannerism, and in every case their eyes were open; while, of course, the movements of their features as they laughed and talked by itself disposes of the suggestion of a set of masks, should the most unreasonable of sceptics have such an idea in mind, and should he also have such a strange opinion of human nature as to imagine that anyone would lavish free hospitality on a stranger for the sole satisfaction of tricking him.

The guide then announced the coming of Betty and asked us to sing one of her favourite songs. We sang *I'll Walk Beside You*, in the middle of which a tall slim figure emerged from the curtain and stood silently in view.

I rose from my chair and walked up to the figure, taking the extended hand in mine. I examined the hand, and it was just like Betty's and quite unlike the medium's. I stared into the face, and recognized my wife. We spoke to each other, though what we said I cannot remember, for I was deeply stirred and so was she and her voice was incoherent with emotion.

"Can he kiss you?" someone asked, and Betty murmured, "Yes." I then kissed her on the lips which were warm, soft, and natural. Thereupon she bent her head and commenced to weep, and in a moment or two she sank. I watched her form right down to the level the floor at my feet where it dissolved, the last wisp of it being drawn within the cabinet.

After I had resumed my seat, there was a pause, perhaps to allow me to recover some of my lost composure; and then the circle guide announced another visitor for me, giving the name 'John Fletcher', and saying that he was a clergyman who had been helping to inspire my book – perhaps the 'clergyman guide' referred to by the male medium in Chapter III, but of whose authenticity I was distinctly dubious.

A tall black-bearded figure then appeared, and when I reached him he gave my hand a very powerful hearty grip, expressed his delight at this meeting between us and my realization at last of his own reality, discussed the book with me, declared that the work was now complete, bade me a cordial farewell, and vanished in the usual manner.

If I once doubted the existence of guides, how can I do so now?

I have told my tale baldly, without any dramatizing or sentimental frills; it must surely be a pathetically warped mind, which cannot supply such omissions from its own imagination.

Footnote: - *There are a couple of mistaken identities in this extract, marked by the numbers.*

(1) Because we were introduced to him en masse just minutes before the sitting started, my father was mistakenly remembered as one of Mrs Shipman's parents, whereas only her mother, Mrs Hildred was present. Her father, Sam Hildred, was a regular communicator from the Spirit world.

(2) 'Aunt Gladys' should, of course, be 'Aunt Agg' about whom you will have already read. Gladys is Mrs Shipman's first name.

(3) 'Buckie' is the name of a town in Scotland where he had previously had a sitting with a Mrs.D. (Tom Harrison)

Lightning Source UK Ltd.
Milton Keynes UK
UKHW03f0932260318
320045UK00001B/20/P